BIG MACS & OUR PENSIONS

Who Gets McDonald's Profits?

ROBERT F. ABBOTT
Word Engines Press
Airdrie, Canada

Word Engines Press

Abbott, Robert F.

Big Macs & Our Pensions: Who Gets McDonald's Profits?

ISBN 978-0-9683287-6-7

Table of Contents

Introduction:
The Ownership Revolution

Ever sit over a Big Mac in McDonald's, watching order after order fly over the counter, and wonder who makes all the profits? You might presume those profits end up in the wallets of millionaires; after all, that's the way it always goes, right?

But....

The McDonald's Corporation mostly belongs to working people, middle-class citizens. That's you and me and hundreds of millions of others around the world.

Few of us became owners because we wanted a piece of the company or its profits. Instead, becoming owners was a side-effect of saving for retirement. But what a side effect! It turned out to be what I call the Ownership Revolution.

Over the past 60 years or so (depending on which country you live in), ownership of big corporations has shifted from rich people to working people. At the beginning of the Ownership Revolution, the rich owned almost all of the stock in big companies. Today, that's reversed, with the majority of stocks in most big corporations belonging to working, or middle class people, through pension funds and mutual funds.

Put another way, we see working people who need to fund and grow their retirement income, and we see companies that need to sell stock to expand. When these two sides began satisfying the needs of the other, a new era of corporate growth and better retirement incomes emerged.

But what about the rich you ask, the 1% as some would call them? Well, we may have less money per person than the rich, but we really outnumber them. When hundreds of millions of us contribute modest amounts each payday, the sums quickly multiply into the billions and trillions.

As Davis, Lukomnik, and Pitt-Watson put it in their book, *The New Capitalists: How Citizen Investors are Reshaping the Corporate Agenda,* "Who are these new capitalists we're talking about?

Corporate power used to be wielded by wealthy tycoons or by the state.... in North America, Europe, Japan, and increasingly throughout the world, the owners of multinational corporations are the tens of millions of working people who have their pensions and other life savings invested through funds in shares of the world's largest companies. Their nest eggs constitute majority ownership of our corporate world. Each pensioner owns a tiny sliver of vast numbers of companies." (Harvard Business School Press, page xi)

According to nasdaq.com (December 18, 2013), institutional investors (primarily pension funds and mutual funds) and mutual funds owned 65% of McDonald's shares. So, we will presume working people own at least two-thirds, and perhaps more, of McDonald's shares. I say presume because some millionaires may have stakes in pension or mutual funds, and at the same time, some middle class people buy McDonald's stock on their own.

Ownership of stock in big corporations has two dimensions: first, sharing in the profits, and second, controlling operations. We'll focus on the profits in *Big Macs & Our Pensions,* but it's worth noting we also share control, indirectly, through the pension fund trustees we elect, and as individuals by buying and selling specific mutual funds.

The dean of business thinkers, Peter F. Drucker, has written, "The rise of pension funds as dominant owners and and lenders represents one of the most startling power shifts in economic history." (*The Pension Fund Revolution,* Transaction Publishers, 1996, page 208)

In this booklet, we explore the Ownership Revolution through McDonald's shares. I chose McDonald's as an example because of its iconic status. Everyone knows the company, almost everyone has eaten its food, and millions have even worked for it. Exploring this revolution through McDonald's also allows us to look at a controversial issue connected with ownership: fast food wages.

Oh yes, we'll also estimate how much of your lunch tab ends up as a profit for McDonald's.

How just another burger joint reinvented itself to create the fast food industry comprises the first part of Chapter 1. Later in the chapter, we explore how McDonald's went from local attraction to worldwide icon, how it makes money selling food and renting real estate, and how it returns money to shareholders through dividends, share buybacks, and reinvestments.

In Chapter 2 we ask why pension funds would buy stocks, and specifically McDonald's stock. After that, a look at the many hats we wear, and at three groups of working people who became owners and now receive McDonald's profits: the California Public Employees Retirement System, the British Columbia Investment Management Corporation (for an international perspective), and a mutual fund, the Vanguard Total Stock Market Index.

In Chapter 3, we examine the contentious issue of fast food wages, through the accusations of a protest campaign and a research report. As owners, we wouldn't want to think our retirement income comes from exploitation. So, we'll listen to the messages of protesters, and analyze. We'll also explore how we, wearing our different hats, will determine the future of fast food wages.

I've written this booklet for those of us who enjoy reading magazines and the editorial pages of newspapers, for those who take an interest in public affairs programs on radio and television, and for those who follow online blogs.

It makes no attempt to serve experts or specialists in any area. In taking this approach, I hope we can all contribute more to political conversations, enjoy a better understanding of the economic world, and help create better public policy.

The author is neither pro- nor anti-McDonald's, and has no connection with the company, other than buying a few Big Mac combos a year. I am an active stock and options trader, but do not own any McDonald's stocks or options, and will not for at least one year after publication of this booklet.

I do not have any direct connection with the pension funds or mutual funds named here, though you will see one indirect connection disclosed later. The funds selected came up somewhat randomly; thousands of others might have illustrated the same points.

Now, let's find out how the Ownership Revolution and the Fast Food Revolution came together to profoundly change our world.

Chapter 1:
From Drive-In to Driving Force

It started as a routine sort of restaurant story. Richard and Maurice (informally known as Dick and Mac) McDonald, the sons of Irish immigrants, opened The Airdrome restaurant in Monrovia, California in 1937. Three years later, they moved it to San Bernardino, California.

Like some other restaurants of the time, it provided car service to capitalize on the growing number of automobiles. Customers pulled up and parked, carhops arrived and took their orders; the orders were custom cooked in the restaurant kitchen, and then delivered to the customers by the carhops. When they finished, customers flashed their headlights; carhops collected their empty trays, dishes, and cutlery, and took them back inside for cleaning and stacking.

Customers liked this novel and convenient approach to eating. For restaurant owners though, the system had costly drawbacks as you can imagine. Providing service outside the restaurant took extra time and labor, dishes, cups, and cutlery would get broken or lost more often, and teenage boys parked for hours to flirt with the carhops.

Nevertheless, this operation satisfied the McDonalds for several years, as the business grew. Success meant living in a 25-room mansion and three new Cadillacs a year (one each for the unmarried Maurice, Richard, and Richard's wife). The money to fund this lifestyle came from a menu that featured several barbeque dishes, but hamburgers and cheeseburgers made up 80% of their sales (Encyclopedia.jrank.org/articles/pages/6307).

Rethinking the Restaurant Model

By 1948, the brothers had figured out how they would deal with the drawbacks of their car-centric restaurant, and gain an edge in pricing too.

They built the new model on what they called the Speedee Service

System. While the earlier McDonald's operation reflected the automobile *driving* revolution, Speedee reflected the *manufacturing* revolution that led to mass production of cars on assembly lines.

Henry Ford, you will recall, introduced the modern assembly line at his Detroit car factory in 1913. Productivity shot up when Ford introduced the line, and it quickly became the standard for manufacturing of all types of goods. 35 years later, in 1948, the McDonald brothers brought the same thinking to restaurants. They temporarily closed their doors, and began to renovate.

The restaurant reopened with a radically slimmed menu: rather than the traditional array of breakfast, lunch, and dinner selections, diners had to choose from just a handful of items, including burgers, fries, and drinks. What's more, customers could eat everything on the menu with just their fingers.

In the cooking area, unskilled production workers replaced skilled short-order cooks, just as unskilled laborers replaced skilled mechanics in car building. One person cooked burgers, and burgers only, while another specialized in french fries, and so on. The art of cooking also disappeared, as each worker rigidly followed a set of instructions for his or her area.

Beyond the kitchen, staff no longer went out to cars. Instead, every customer had to come inside and stand at a cash register to place an order. When their orders arrived, customers found their food wrapped in paper. No more dishes, no more cutlery. And at the new McDonald's customers found no tables, counters, or chairs; they had to eat everything outside the restaurant.

At the same time, the McDonalds allowed customers to see right into the kitchen, to see their food being prepared. That neatly tied into the brothers' obsession with cleanliness. The kitchen always remained clean, a characteristic the company and corporation maintained as they grew from one location to more than 34-thousand.

Customers gave up selection and service; instead they got fast and cheap, with orders assembled and placed in front of them in literally a minute. What was the price? Diners got a burger for 15 cents, about half the usual price, and corresponding prices for the other menu items. They loved it!

A key to the new, low-price strategy was lower labor costs. The brothers eliminated the wait staff and the short order cooks, both groups comprising skilled or at least semi-skilled staff. In their place, they hired unskilled workers and gave them just enough training to do one specific task. Essentially anyone could do any job in the restaurant with minimal training, so wages started low and stayed low.

It's critical to note that the brothers brought a low-price business model to the restaurant industry. Today, many of us take for granted our access to low-priced food of reasonable quality. Before McDonald's and the emergence of the fast food industry, low-priced usually meant places called *greasy spoons,* eateries with food of dubious quality and even more dubious standards of cleanliness.

In moving to self-serve, Richard and Maurice confused many customers at first; some still sat in the parking lot and honked their horns. But, soon the low prices, near-instant delivery of their food, and transparent cleanliness won them over.

For the McDonald brothers, the low-price strategy led to another important development. With the carhops gone, teenage boys stopped hanging around. Instead, families became the core customers. As author and McDonald's critic Eric Schlosser concedes in **Fast Food Nation: The Dark Side of the All-American Meal,** families lined up at the new McDonald's, and he quotes McDonald's historian John F. Love, "Working-class families could finally afford to feed their kids restaurant food." (HarperCollins, 2002, page 20)

With that acceptance, both existing and new customers became loyal patrons, and before long lineups began to appear. Along with customers came curious competitors, suppliers, and entrepreneurs.

Expanding the Vision

Visits from entrepreneurs led to the first, hesitating steps toward the formation of a chain. The first franchise restaurant opened in 1952, and seven more appeared in the following two years. Yet, the

McDonalds showed limited interest in expanding and it seemed the chain had gone as far as it would go.

That changed with the arrival of milkshake-machine salesman Ray Kroc. He first visited a McDonald's in 1954 and left, according to the corporation's website, *stunned*. He came in impressed because the company placed a big order for milkshake machines. What stayed with him was the efficiency and effectiveness of the food assembly line.

He made time to talk with the brothers. Kroc, like the McDonald brothers, came from outside the traditional food service culture and had a history as a maverick. In 1917, soon after the United States entered World War I, the 15-year old Kroc lied about his age so he could join the Red Cross as an ambulance driver.

The war ended before Kroc could see active service, and he briefly went back to high school. After dropping out of school, he went to work at the Lily-Tulip Cup Co., where, as an ***Entrepreneur*** magazine profile (October 8, 2008) notes, he proved ambitious and hardworking. He set sales records and quickly became a top salesperson.

Through his work at Lily-Tulip Cup Co., Kroc met the inventor of a five-spindle milkshake machine, the Multimixer. This machine, like the Speedee Service System which would follow, offered major productivity gains. Seeing the milkshake machine's efficiency and potentially lucrative sales commissions, Kroc went to work selling them.

By the 1950s, changes in the industry led to declining sales of Multimixers,with one notable exception: an order for eight machines at once. That order came, of course, from McDonald's. Curious about the restaurant, both because of the milkshake machine order and word of mouth, Kroc traveled to California to call on the McDonald brothers.

As with the Multimixer, Kroc saw a money-making opportunity, this time in repeating the McDonald's system over and over. The brothers expressed little enthusiasm; they sold rights to the Speedee Service System for $1,000 per location and did not foresee much franchise growth.

They pointed out they did not want to do it themselves, and their franchising agent had quit. Kroc proposed to represent them and after a handshake deal, won exclusive rights to sell the method. For each sale, Kroc would get $950 plus 1.9% of gross sales (good2work.com/article/19392).

Kroc quickly opened an outlet of his own and sold a number of franchises, only to discover he had locked himself into a poor proposition after paying expenses and royalties. As he grappled with that problem, Harry Sonnenborn, a Vice-President at Tastee Freeze and a man with an idea, called on him.

Sonnenborn believed that real estate, not food, would provide the foundation for a fast food empire. The general idea, one still at the core of McDonald's strategy today, was to buy sites and lease them to the franchisees.

Franchisees would pay a fee or a percentage of their sales, whichever was greater. With its unique real estate model, outstanding marketing, and the Speedee Service System the McDonald's Corporation grew quickly and profitably, but not smoothly. Kroc and the McDonald brothers frequently fought, and in 1961 Kroc bought them out for $2.7-million.

For the McDonald brothers, it ended badly, despite the buyout. They continued on in their original location, under the name **Big M**. But continuing friction prompted Kroc to open a conventional, competing McDonald's outlet nearby. The original restaurant soon closed, and the historic building itself was torn down.

Kroc, meanwhile, moved on. To grow and achieve the potential he envisioned, the company had to go public. It needed capital (money from investors), a lot of it, and that could only come from the stock market. In 1965, he took the company public, offering shares at $22.50 each.

McDonald's Today

As we know, that move gave Kroc the capital he needed to create the larger-than-life corporation we know today. And to see what today's company does, we'll look at the McDonald's Corporation's 2012 Annual Report. For the doubters among us, yes, you can, or should be able to trust what management says in the document; any incorrect or misleading statements could lead to severe penalties including jail time.

The company tells us it operated 34,480 restaurants at the end of 2012. As you'll recall, the McDonald brothers had eight locations in 1954 when Ray Kroc appeared. Franchisees operated about 81% of those 34,480 restaurants, and the McDonald's Corporation operated the other 19%.

From a shareholder's perspective, having at least some company-operated restaurants makes sense. These facilities provide an eye on the business and the industry. Company officials also get first-hand intelligence about consumer and civic issues. More importantly, though, company restaurants provide a lab of sorts, a lab in which management can try new products and new operational tactics. Since Speedee arrived in 1948, the company has continued to search for new and better ways of preparing and serving food. It also continues to experiment with menu items, some of which survive, some which come back from time to time, and some that disappear forever.

What's more, it keeps testing different prices within its menu. We note in the *Management Discussion and Analysis* section, discussion about something the corporation calls a strategic pricing tool; "In our Company-operated restaurants, we manage menu board prices to ensure value at all price points, increase profitability and mitigate inflation, all while trying to grow guest counts. In order to accomplish these objectives, we utilize a strategic pricing tool that balances price and product mix. Franchisees also have access...."

We might think the company simply charges whatever prices it wants. But that assumes fast food companies enjoy the status of price setters (also called price makers) rather than price takers.

Price setting companies enjoy the luxury of deciding how much to charge for the products or services they sell. But this business luxury usually only applies to monopolies (post offices, for example), companies with strong patents (such as technology companies), and firms with exceptional competencies (design at Apple).

Price takers on the other hand, take what they can get, what the market will give them. That includes the highly competitive food services industry. What's more, it does not simply mean a McDonald's meal matches or beats the value of a Wendy's meal; instead, it means pricing within what we might call an ecosystem of food prices. If the price of a fast food burger goes up, customers may decide to go to a casual dining restaurant instead, or to pick up hamburger patties and buns at a supermarket.

Of course, every fast food company has some limited discretion in its pricing, particularly when it combines products into packages or innovates with new products. Fast food outlets may only gain a few cents per item but when you combine ultra-high volume with a few cents here and a few cents there, it adds up quickly.

Turning to franchises, we note franchise operations give the company an entrepreneurial perspective and dynamic. 28,000 independently operated outlets can generate a lot of ideas. The Big Mac, for example, came from a franchisee, as did many other products and productivity ideas.

From a share owner's perspective, franchise operations significantly reduce the amount of capital needed for each new location, allowing the company to expand more quickly than it would otherwise. And, as we'll discuss in more detail later, public companies need to keep growing constantly.

Generally speaking, the Corporation owns and manages the real estate while franchisees manage the local businesses. A major part of the revenue stream from franchisees covers rental of the property. As we noted earlier, real estate provides one of the main pillars of the company's success. With that in mind, take note of this sentence in the Management Discussion and Analysis, "Revenues from conventional franchised restaurants include rent and royalties based on a percent of sales along with minimum rent payments and initial fees."

The phrases, *minimum rate payments* and *initial fees,* caught my eye. In other words, we shareholders will get our money, or at least a chunk of it, even if the franchisee does not make a profit. Put in more technical terms, franchisees shoulder a significant amount of business risk the corporation would otherwise bear. As shareholders, we like that.

The corporation's logic about franchising goes like this: The company sees itself primarily as a franchisor, and "...franchising is important to delivering great, locally-relevant customer experiences and driving profitability." To that it adds, "...directly operating restaurants is paramount to being a credible franchisor and is essential to providing Company personnel with restaurant operations experience." So, as we noted earlier, the McDonald's Corporation created a package, if you will, in which the company maintains its roots in order to remain an effective franchisor.

In the broader perspective, McDonald's also focuses intently on its suppliers. In its annual report we see frequent references to the word *alignment*, which refers to the practice of maintaining productive relationships among all the players in its business. That ranges from the companies that grow the food through to the staff who hand the finished meal to you.

Earlier we discussed the conscious creation of a low-price, high-volume business model. To make money with this model the price paid for supplies becomes critical. Paying the right price for commodities, such as meat, buns, and soft drinks becomes as important as offering the right prices to customers. In fact, without good supply management, the company cannot offer competitive prices to customers.

Geographical segments get lots of attention in the annual report, which is not surprising for a company both hailed and flailed as the poster child of globalization. The corporation divides its world this way: United States, Europe, APMEA (Asia/Pacific, Middle East, and Africa), as well as what's known as Other Countries & Corporate (Latin America, Canada, and something called corporate activities).

With operations in 119 countries, currency exchange rates can make a significant difference to the company's bottom line. For the purposes of measuring and managing consistently, McDonald's uses what it calls *constant currencies* (which we won't even attempt to explain here). Simply remember that currency rates among countries do matter, just as they do when we as individuals travel or holiday in another country.

Regardless of location, every restaurant needs to improve its results every month, quarter, and year. The industry-wide measure by which they're assessed is called *Comparable Sales* and investors of all stripes watch this number carefully. In addition, McDonald's also considers *Comparable Guest Counts* a key number. Taken together, the two numbers allow the Corporation to know whether each location continues to grow or not.

With growth a company experiences upward pressure on its share price and brings in new money for expansion. Growth keeps investors happy, since they want to increase their nest eggs and it produces jobs for workers, bonuses for management, and higher taxes for governments. Everyone likes growth.

So, How Much did We Make?

Now let's take a look at some key results posted in 2012. We can start with Comparable Sales, which rose about 3%, an increase, but only about half of the 5.6% posted in 2011. Guest Counts increased 1.6%, again about half of the increase posted in 2011.

And, just a couple of more numbers now. First, it had revenue of just over $27 and a half billion.

Take off almost $19 billion for expenses, and you're left with operating income of $8.6 billion.

From that, deduct costs for interest, non-operating expenses, a provision for income taxes ($2.6 billion) and you're left with a net income, or profit, of $5.465 billion.

And what did McDonald's do with the money that flowed from operations, from the money it has borrowed ($13.6 billion at the end of 2012), and from the money it earned as profits?

First, it returned about $5.5 billion to shareholders, through dividends and share buybacks (from an owner's perspective, share buybacks mean future profits are divided among fewer owners, a good thing for investors, but not realized as quickly as dividends).

It also invested just over $3 billion in what financial people call capital expenditures, or capex in everyday jargon. Of that amount, about $1.3 billion went into the development of 1,439 new restaurants (it also closed 469). Traditional new restaurants in the U.S.A. cost an average of $2.9 million, according to the annual report. That covers land, buildings, and equipment.

Another $1.6 billion went into what the company calls reimaging of existing restaurants. Think of that as remodeling with a particular style. Whatever we call it, new restaurants and remodeled restaurants sell more, in the near term and the long term.

What's the profit on your lunch?

With that covered, let's go off on a short tangent, and do a back-of-the-napkin calculation on how much profit McDonald's makes when we eat in one of its restaurants. We divide the profit of $5.465 billion by its gross income of $27.567 billion and get just under 20%. So, on your $10 lunch tab, let's say the company makes about $2.

That amount will vary from day to day (remember the strategic pricing tool?), whether you eat in a company-operated or franchisee-operated restaurant, and a dozen other factors. But, 20% gives us a rough guide.

If you belong to a pension plan, contribute to a mutual fund, or pay into a whole life insurance policy, you and your fellow plan members will share in part of that $2. As we noted, funds of working people own about two-thirds of McDonald's shares. So let's say collectively we get back about $1.32 (66%), although the actual number will vary.

All of this has been a grand generalization, of course. The amount that comes back to us through franchise restaurants will differ from what we get back from a company-owned restaurant. And, since literally thousands of franchisees exist, we expect differences from restaurant to restaurant, country to country, and so on.

Summing up this chapter, we've seen how two brothers with a vision reinvented the burger business, and how a man with a vision for expansion took it to the world. In the process, we saw the emergence of the low-price, high-volume business model, one which depends on low-priced labor.

We also looked at McDonald's as a mature business, one which generates revenue from food sales in company-owned restaurants and from fees and rents collected from franchise-operated restaurants. And we looked at how it allocated its income, to dividends, share buybacks, and reinvestments in new and existing facilities.

Big picture: Through pension funds and mutual funds, we invest our money in corporations like McDonald's and in return expect a steady stream of income in return.

Chapter 2:
Meet the New Owners

Why would a pension fund buy stocks? Aren't they risky? You might think it a good thing to collect the income from a public corporation like McDonald's, but wonder why your pension fund or mutual fund invests in stocks in the first place.

Your grandfather's pension fund did not invest in stocks of any kind, but yours does. What's changed? Originally many, if not most employers paid pensions out of their earnings (profits), or bought annuities, a form of life insurance, for their employees. Later, they added bonds, which are loans to governments or companies with good credit records. Both annuities and bonds provided safe pensions for employees, but paying out of earnings did not.

Overall, several things have changed since grandfather's day, prompting employers to take a fresh look at using stocks in their pension plans. First, pension coverage expanded from salaried to hourly employees, especially since the Second World War. In a manufacturing plant, for example, this would mean employees on the shop floor would gain coverage already provided to senior office staff.

After World War II, unions began asking to have pensions included in contract negotiations. In the United States, they officially got the green light in a key National Labor Relations Bureau ruling of 1948. In many other countries, unions gained or assumed that right around the same time. Union involvement in pension negotiations led to both the inclusion of more employees, and promises of higher pensions in the future.

As a result of these and other changes, the people in charge of paying pensions began to foresee a crunch: too much money going out and not enough coming in. They believed that stocks could close or reduce the gap, because of higher returns.

In addition, academic and other research in the 1950s and beyond showed fund managers could reduce risk by adding stocks to a portfolio of only bonds. Harry Markowitz and his Modern Portfolio Theory led the way in establishing that diversity reduced the amount of price fluctuation (volatility) or risk. In other words, a portfolio with stocks as well as bonds would prove safer than a portfolio made up of bonds alone.

This development flew in the face of conventional wisdom. Since the great stock market crash of 1929 almost all fund managers assumed stocks posed too much risk. Now, they were learning, from both academic studies and practical investing experience, that adding stocks to a fund actually reduced the odds of losing money.

These and other factors led pension fund managers to slowly begin adding stocks to their portfolios. Now, managers often have 40% or more of their funds allocated to stocks. In mutual funds, which gained wider acceptance in the 1950s, equity funds (all stocks or a high proportion of stocks) delivered above-average returns to investors.

The inclusion of equity, or stocks, in a retirement portfolio helps most of us. Higher returns on fund portfolios mean we pay less for the same amount of retirement income. Alternatively, it means we receive more retirement income for the same value of contributions. And, if you get a pension from your work, it means employers pay less, so our wages can go a bit higher.

Second, why would pension funds buy McDonald's stock specifically? McDonald's became part of the Ownership Revolution in 1965, when the company went public, when it first offered shares to all investors and institutions. It's unlikely many pension funds invested in McDonald's in 1965, and those that did likely bought a modest number of shares. Then, as now, pension funds preferred to put most of their money into big businesses with proven track records.

McDonald's no doubt began developing that track record, and a good relationship with both pension fund and mutual fund managers the following year, when it announced its first stock split. Investors received 3 shares of McDonald's for every 2 shares they held on March 29, 1966. Since then, the stock has split 12 times, and still risen to the $100 a share range in 2013.

Both corporations and investors like stock splits. A split reduces the price per share, making shares more affordable to smaller investors.

Generally, a lower-priced stock will enjoy more demand, and that demand will pull up the price per share, satisfying both investors and the issuing corporation.

Investors and fund managers also like stocks that pay a dividend. A dividend is a distribution of the corporation's profits to its owners, the shareholders. McDonald's joined the dividend club on May 14, 1976 with a two and a half cent per share payment (see the company's website, Dividends page, October 22, 2013). Now, two and a half cents per share may not sound like much, but when you own hundreds of thousands or even millions of shares, as many funds do, it adds up very quickly.

The company has increased its dividend every year since then. That makes it part of a special elite in the investment world: the S&P Dow Jones Indices recognizes corporations that have increased their dividends every year for at least 20 years as Dividend Aristocrats (also listed by some services as Dividend Champions, or something similar). According to S&P Dow Jones Indices, only 83 out of the many thousands of U. S. public companies enjoyed a place on that list on December 3, 2013 (http://us.spindices.com/indices/strategy/sp -high-yield -dividend -aristocrats -index).

The introduction of a dividend also sends an important signal to the market, and especially to investors and fund managers. The corporation is saying it is confident it can grow and increase its earnings in coming years.

Third, investors buy McDonald's in hopes of making capital gains. Buying shares for one price and selling them later for a higher price provides a capital gain (or a capital loss if the share price is lower at the time of sale). Those who bought 100 McDonald's shares in 1965 would have invested $2,250; those same shares would have had a value of $6.6-million on December 31, 2012 (according to figures from the company's website, Stock Split page, October 22, 2013; these values account for stock splits, but do not reference inflation).

In 1985, the company became part of the Dow Jones Industrial Average because of its large capitalization (number of shares multiplied by the price per share). With its inclusion in this index, it gained added corporate respectability and a greater following among conservative investors, including pension funds. That would have cemented its place as a member of the investing establishment, even without its rapid growth.

Growth matters in a world where inflation consistently takes a toll on our savings. Over the past century, few demons have ravaged savings as badly as inflation. We've seen examples of acute cases, such as Germany between the two World Wars and a number of South American countries in the latter half of the 20th Century. But even in the best-managed economies, low-level, chronic inflation has led to despair among many retirees.

Yes, using stocks as protection against inflation comes at a price; sometimes these investments go bad and we lose part or all of our capital. But, managers and academics alike agree that stocks belong in every effective retirement savings plan. For now at least, it's simply the best hedge against inflation we have.

Combine a steadily growing dividend and a steadily growing stock price, and you can understand why we see big investments by funds. They want strong, predictable growth and McDonald's delivers it.

Who is "We"?

So far, I've used the word *we* rather loosely, using it to describe those of us who own a stake in big business through our pension funds, mutual funds, and other retirement savings vehicles.

As you'll see in the sections ahead, *we* gets complicated in real life. While we are owners, we also wear the hats of employees, suppliers, consumers, citizens, taxpayers, voters, and more. Sometimes those roles align but they can also conflict with one another.

And even if you haven't yet contributed to a pension plan or mutual fund, you're still one of *us* because you may well inherit ownership in a mutual fund from older family members. And don't overlook the fact that your parents may belong to a pension plan; until relatively recently, younger generations paid (if they could) to care for older family members who could no longer work.

Many of us relate, or have related in the past, to McDonald's as consumers, but you'll now see that's a limited view. As consumers we want the lowest prices, and as owners we prefer higher prices. At the same time, as citizens and taxpayers, we want fast food businesses that provide jobs and tax revenue without harming our health.

In addition, I've used the terms *working people* and *middle class people* rather loosely and interchangeably throughout. That's intentional. Generally I think of working people, even the working poor, as current or future contributors to pension funds, mutual funds, or both. At the upper end, I generally expect the richer among us to not have jobs, and consequently not be part of pension funds. Similarly, I expect the rich to invest directly in stocks and bonds, whether on their own or through a financial adviser, rather than mutual funds.

Rather vague I know, but also a consequence of the Ownership Revolution, which defines us by our arms-length investments. As we'll see shortly, California's public employee pension plan includes occupations ranging from school custodians to supreme court judges.

Regardless of our class status, we all wear many hats, something to remember as we read about some of the owners of McDonald's. But before we do that, try this rhetorical quiz question: If a government sues tobacco companies and wins, which of our hats win and which of our hats lose?

California Public Employees' Retirement System

No matter where in the world you live, many public employees in the State of California hope you enjoyed your meal at McDonald's and that you'll come back soon (actually, I'm putting words in their mouths, words with which some would undoubtedly disagree).

That's because shares in McDonald's make an important contribution to the pensions of public employees in that state (and in many other places as well). California Public Employees' Retirement System, or CalPERS as it's commonly known, represented 1,678,996 active and retired civil servants as of June 30, 2013 (unless otherwise noted, all facts and figures below came from the CALPERS website on October 23, 2013).

Of that number, about a third have already retired or receive some form of allowance from the pension fund. What is called the average monthly service allowance (pensions and other benefits) averages out to $2,629 per recipient.

CalPERS does not represent all public employees, but does take in a significant number employed by the State, by school boards, and local public agencies. The roster of occupations within the plan ranges from school custodians to Supreme Court of California judges.

We note as well that members and state-appointed delegates manage the fund. Starting at the top, Rob Feckner, the President of CalPERS Board of Administration, holds a day job described as glazing specialist, someone who fixes windows and glass. Earlier, he worked as a school bus driver and instructional assistant for special needs students.

Other members of the board that manages the fund include an academic at California State University, a bookstore operations coordinator at a community college, a senior human resources manager for the state government, a political aide, a lawyer, an investment specialist, a chief financial officer, a senior trade unionist, the State Treasurer, a financial analyst, and, the president of a municipal district.

This board, the Board of Administration, hires and oversees professional managers, investment agencies, and other services needed to run the pension plan. In addition to pensions, it also provides health service plans for about 1.3 million members. It has 2,726 employees and a head office located in Sacramento, California.

CalPERS is a big organization, obviously, and a big buyer and seller of stocks. One of the investments it uses to meet its commitments is McDonald's stock. It owned just over 2.75-million shares on

September 30, 2013 (http://www.nasdaq.com/symbol/mcd/institution al-holdings?page=3).

You'll recall we earlier talked about dividends adding up when you have a lot of shares; that applies here. Take the December 2013 quarterly dividend payout by McDonald's, 81 cents, and multiply that by 2.75-million, and you'll see CalPERS would collect $2.23 million. That's for one quarter (of a fiscal year); annualized, it works out to $8.92-million.

For another perspective, divide that $8.92 million by $2,629, the average monthly service allowance and you'll see dividends provide enough income to make 3,393 monthly pension payments in a year (not that I'm trying to make any direct connection between specific dividends and specific pension payments).

Looking at numbers from the 2012 annual report, we see fund members paid just over $125 million to buy these shares, and at the date of this report (June 30, 2012) had a value of of more than $260 million. A quick eyeballing of the numbers will tell you the shares have more than doubled in price; good news for these owners.

The McDonald's holding is just one of literally thousands of assets owned by California's public employees through their pension fund. But it underlines how working people, each contributing just a small amount each month, can collectively buy big stakes in big corporations.

British Columbia Investment Management Corporation

If you drive 721 miles north from Sacramento, the home base of CalPERS, you'll come to the Canadian border. Just across the line you'll see British Columbia (B.C.), a province within the Canadian federation. About 4.5-million residents live in the province.

Like California, it has public employees with a strong interest in the fortunes of the McDonald's Corporation. The British Columbia

Investment Management Corporation (BCIMC) invests on behalf of some 500-thousand public employees (including some members of my immediate and extended family). In addition, it manages insurance and benefit funds for more than 2.2-million workers (unless otherwise noted, all facts and figures came from the BCIMC website on October 23, 2013).

As its organizational profile notes, "Our investment activities help to finance the retirement benefits of more than 500,000 plan members including university and college instructors and staff, municipal employees, healthcare workers, firefighters, police officers, public servants, teachers, and....").

That plan held more than $100 billion worth of assets, including almost $108 million worth of McDonald's stock on March 31, 2013. The holding is one of its largest, representing slightly more than 1% of the full portfolio.

But, B.C.'s government employees won't feel disappointed if you cross the street and eat at Burger King. They also own more than $10.5 million worth of Burger King stock. Prefer just a coffee and a light snack? No problem, they also own more than $52 million worth of Starbucks. Or perhaps you'd like something slightly more upscale, like Red Lobster or the Olive Garden; they own nearly $7-million worth of stock in Darden Restaurants Inc. (Darden owns these two chains plus a half dozen more restaurant brands). Given that these public employees own stock in literally thousands of corporations, you can eat at all sorts of places and help finance their retirement.

Getting back to McDonald's, B.C.'s public employees own 1,065,588 shares. Assuming their holdings remain the same as listed on March 31st, they would have collected dividends valued at $863,126 when McDonald's paid out its dividend on December 16, 2013. Over four quarters (a year), they would collect $3,452,505 in dividends.

I include British Columbia Investment Management Corporation here to highlight the international scope of investment in McDonald's. Many other pension funds and mutual funds hail from beyond the United States. According to NASDAQ (Ownership &

Insider Trades, November 18, 2013), Norges Bank, Norway's Central Bank, owns more than 8 million shares, on behalf of the Government Pension Fund of Norway.

We know McDonald's has become an icon of globalization for consumers, but it also helps fund retirement incomes worldwide too.

Mutual Funds & ETFs

While many of us do not belong to pension funds, we still may share in the ownership of McDonald's. Some of us may own a piece of the company through our investments in the stock itself, while others among us may own our bits through mutual funds and exchange-traded funds (ETFs).

Given that the price per share has hovered at or around $100 for some time, few of us likely own them outright. But, many of us can afford to buy through mutual funds or ETFs that hold the company's shares.

Ownership through mutual funds and ETFs occurs in several ways. It happens directly when we buy units of a fund for ourselves through a sales person, a stock broker, or other channel. Some of us do this on our own and some of us buy units of the fund as part of a benefits package at work.

In the latter case, units in a mutual fund or ETF are bought for us if we belong to a defined contribution plan. In these plans, an employer, an employee, or both, contribute toward the employee's retirement income.

Mutual funds have a special place in the Ownership Revolution, which saw working people buy up shares in big corporations. According to one industry source, "Ownership of mutual funds by U.S. households has grown significantly over the past three decades. Forty-four percent of all U.S. households owned mutual funds in 2011, compared with less than 6 percent in 1980. The estimated 90 million individuals who owned mutual funds in 2011 included many different types of people across all age and income groups with a variety of financial goals." (2012 Investment Company Fact Book, Investment Company Institute, 52nd Edition, 2012, page 85).

We can say these 90 million investors have a variety of financial goals, but as the Investment Company Institute also notes, 73% of them listed retirement income as a primary goal. And 94% included retirement savings as one of their goals.

Some call the expansion of mutual funds the democratization of investing. As President Paul Schott Stevens of the Investment Company Institute told the 2005 Mutual Funds and Investment Management Conference, "After centuries of being an elite privilege, investing has grown to become a mass opportunity. America has taken an extraordinary leap forward in creating an 'Ownership Society'.... Mutual funds are one of the principal reasons." (http://www.ici.org/pressroom/speeches/05_mfimc_steven s_spch).

With that perspective, let's look at one of the mutual funds that bought McDonald's stock for its unit-holders (think of a unit-holder as the equivalent of a shareholder; shares in a mutual fund are called units, hence the name).

The biggest mutual fund owner of McDonald's shares is the Vanguard Total Stock Market Index. It holds nearly 15 million shares, giving its unit-holders a nearly 1.5% share of all McDonald's stock. Looking at the fund's website, we see it had $296.4 billion (more than a quarter of a trillion dollars) in net fund assets on November 30, 2011 (https://personal.vanguard.com/us/fundssnap shot?FundId=0085&FundIntExt=INT).

To give you a sense of the size of the fund, consider this: even though it owns almost 15-million shares of McDonald's worth more than $1.4 billion (at the close of trading on November 30, 2013), shares of McDonald's do not even make its top 10 list of holdings.

If you own units of the Vanguard Total Stock Market Index, you receive a quarterly distribution (roughly the equivalent of a dividend). The most recent distribution, on September 23, 2013) paid 19.6 cents per unit, a fraction of which will have originated with dividends from McDonald's.

If the numbers make your eyes glaze over, it's okay, we're past them now. And, they're secondary to the main point: You, your family, or your friends might well participate in ownership of McDonald's through a mutual fund or ETF, as well as a through a pension fund.

Turning to the bigger picture, we see how the profits of corporations make their way to pension funds and mutual funds. From there the profits get passed along to us; enhancing our retirement incomes.

In some, if not many cases, we will receive more retirement income support from corporations than from governments. We might also say that one of the unintended consequences of the Ownership Revolution has been to turn big business into an instrument for social policy.

We're accustomed to looking at jobs and taxes as the two most important social functions of big business. But the time has come to add a third; retirement income support. Although many among us may not realize it, we have come to depend on corporate profits to support our current or future standards of living.

To cite a recent example, after the major BP oil spill in the Gulf of Mexico a British newspaper, The Telegraph reported, "BP's position at the top of the London Stock Exchange and its previous reliability have made it a bedrock of almost every pension fund in the country, meaning its value is crucial to millions of workers. The firm's dividend payments, which amount to more than £7 billion a year, account for £1 in every £6 paid out in dividends to British pension pots." (June 9, 2010) We might argue about a failure to properly diversify among British pension funds, but the case still underlines the social utility of corporate profits.

So we have working people investing in big corporations through pension funds and mutual funds; corporations using those investments to grow, leading to bigger dividends and higher share prices for the people who made the investments, and everyone's happy. Well, not quite everyone, as we'll see in the next chapter.

To recap, you'll recall from Chapter 1 that the McDonald brothers essentially invented the fast food industry, and they did it in part by eliminating skilled labor. Their low-price, high-volume business model builds on low-priced labor. We also saw that this model works well for investors, providing them with dividends, capital gains, and share buybacks.

In Chapter 2 we've learned that pension funds invest our money in equities, stocks, as well as vehicles that have a reputation for safety, such as government bonds. In addition, individuals invest in equity mutual funds as well as funds with a greater reputation for safety, such as bond funds. Whichever the case, we all want equities/stocks because they help us grow our retirement income.

We also discussed the many hats each of us may wear at any given time: investor, consumer, employee, voter, taxpayer. We met some of the new owners, including public employees and working people around the globe. And we learned how dividends, share buybacks, and capital gains from McDonald's add significantly to their retirement income.

Chapter 3:
Fast Food Fracases

What's called the Fast Food Fight flared up in the United States during the summer of 2013, as activists, trade unionists (primarily the Service Employees International Union), and sympathetic media spoke out, struck, and marched to demand higher wages for employees of McDonald's and other fast food chains.

Only a small fraction of fast food employees participated, but enough to gain sympathetic media coverage. An editorial in the New York Times read, "The Great Recession and the slow recovery have reinforced trends toward inequality and inadequate pay that were evident even before the last downturn. Fast-food workers are fighting back, in just cause." (August 7, 2013).

So, as owners, or at least potential owners, we should find out for ourselves what our company has done, if we have been unjust. After all, we (wearing our shareholder hats) do bear at least some responsibility for the wages of fast food workers.

We expect, but don't know for sure, that this drive has sympathizers around the world; the company now has restaurants in 119 countries. We also know that the fast food business model everywhere works with the low-price, high-volume strategy. So wages everywhere likely match (on a localized basis) the wages paid in the U.S.A.

The demands of this loosely-organized American group focused mainly on wages. Some demanded an immediate increase to $15 an hour, while others asked governments for an increase in minimum wages. Yet others called for improvements in benefits such as health insurance and for more hours of work.

Both protesters and sympathetic media focused on three main claims: (1) the amount of revenue generated by companies like McDonald's, (2) the salaries of executives, and (3) the prices of products sold at fast food restaurants.

Many of us sympathize with the plight of these workers. Speaking personally, not long ago I spent five years working at a job that paid a low wage, a consequence of being an unsuccessful entrepreneur.

Others among us no doubt wear both shareholder and employee hats, while yet others will have family members struggling to survive on low-wage jobs.

Still, it seems little will change as a result of protests and media coverage. Not because of bullheaded resistance by companies like McDonald's, but because the many faces of *we*.

Collectively, we shareholders have set certain relationships between risk and reward. If our return on fast food stocks declines, we will move our capital, our investing money, out of fast food stocks. That, in turn, would lead to more downward pressure on wages, as companies seek to regain previous levels of profitability.

Collectively wearing our shareholder hats, we will not dramatically change our stance on executive pay. We consider growth essential to maintaining our retirement income, and we'll pay a premium to get it if we have to. What's more, many of us saw two previous attempts, through regulation, to constrain executive pay; both backfired and led to higher pay packages rather than lower.

When we put on our voter hats, we quietly tiptoe around the minimum wage issue. Yes, some of us argue it should increase, but collectively we've let our politicians know we don't want increases of any significance. Not that we're unsympathetic, but rather because of concern about unintended consequences including the potential loss of jobs among people who need them most.

Most importantly, though, our consumer hats trump every other hat in our closets. Consumers, including most of us who also own shares directly or indirectly, have voted overwhelmingly for the status quo; for low prices.

Collectively, we've told McDonald's, Walmart, and many companies in the low-price, high-volume market that we like the way they manage their businesses.

When we hand over our cash or credit cards, we tell these companies we want them to keep on doing what they now do. A million critics (to arbitrarily pick a number) may complain, but every day nearly 70 million people pour into McDonald's and vote in favor of its business practices.

Hidden Subsidies?

The wages of fast food workers also hit the news in 2013 with the release of a report claiming American taxpayers pay hidden subsidies to the fast food companies. Here's how an article in the Huffington Post (October 18, 2013) led off, "Taxpayers spend about $7 billion per year to help pay workers who are employed by an industry that rakes in $200 billion annually."

So as people who own, or may own shares in McDonald's, albeit through pension funds or mutual funds, should we ask politicians to fix this? Should we send a protest message to our pension fund trustees or divest our holdings in mutual funds that hold fast food stocks?

Before doing any of those things, let's review the study and the conclusions it reached. We can start by reading the original report titled, *Fast Food, Poverty Wages: The Public Cost of Low-Wage Jobs in the Fast-Food Industry.* It comes from University of California, Berkeley, Center for Labor Research and Education and the University of Illinois at Urbana-Champaign Department of Urban & Regional Planning.

Fast Food, Poverty Wages says, "This paper documents the significant cost to the public resulting from a combination of low wages, part-time work hours and low benefits in fast-food and other low-wage industries." (page 2). Within the world of low-wage industries, it focuses on fast food and says, "The cost for families of front-line fast-food workers averaged nearly $7 billion a year." (page 2).

The report also emphasizes the role of adult employees. It points out, "Overall, 68 percent of the core front-line workers in the fast-food industry are not in school and are single or married adults with or without children. For more than two-thirds of these workers, fast-food wages are an essential component of family income." (page 10).

The researchers and authors of the report meticulously outline their methodology, and define their terms. And they have carefully drawn results from within the parameters.

But, we see a fatal flaw nevertheless. It has to do with the first question any researcher needs to ask before adding, subtracting, or multiplying any numbers: what causes what? Think of it as the academic equivalent of which came first, the chicken or the egg? In the academic world that's not a trivial question since good research always questions the underlying assumptions rigorously.

This principle has relevance in other areas as well. Not long ago, I watched a television quasi-documentary about a doctor in an emergency room. A patient came in suffering a serious head injury and seizures. No one had seen the patient collapse, so the doctor had to determine whether the head injury caused the seizures or the seizures caused the patient to fall and injure her head. No significant treatment could begin until the doctor could distinguish cause from effect.

To confirm or reject the premise behind *Fast Food, Poverty Wages,* we might start by asking if the protesting employees would take other jobs if they could. Since they took to the streets, we have to assume they would. This prompts a second question: why haven't they taken other jobs already?

No other jobs seems the first and mostly likely answer. Other common answers might include not having appropriate skills or experience, they cannot or will not move, or perhaps they do not have suitable clothing (consider Working Gear, a volunteer-run organization in Vancouver, British Columbia, which has the following mission statement on its website, http://www.workinggear.ca, "To relieve poverty by providing interview clothing and/or industry appropriate clothing to low income or unemployed men in search of employment.").

If no other jobs exist for these employees, then the fast food industry provides a job for someone who would otherwise have no job at all. In doing so, the industry helps rather than hurts taxpayers. From a taxpayers' perspective, it's better to pay a portion of public benefits rather than the full amount.

If we consider issues such as lack of skills or experience, inability to move, or lack of appropriate clothing then we could hardly hold the fast food industry responsible. In many cases, a part-time job in fast food, even at low pay, helps overcome these barriers to better-paying employment. We know vast numbers of workers get the first line on their resumes by working in fast food.

As owners, then, we need not apologize for the wages at McDonald's or the other fast food chains. If society (that's all of us, wearing all of our hats) wants better wages for fast food workers, then it must foster new jobs by developing appropriate economic policies.

Corporate profits may look like obvious candidates for funding social causes but as we now know, they already serve a social cause. Using McDonald's as an example, we see it alone contributed $5.5 billion dollars in 2012 to pensions and retirement incomes.

Conclusion:
Two Extraordinary Revolutions

In this booklet, we've had brief but insightful glimpses into two revolutions: one that changed our stake in the world of business, and one that changed the way we eat and think about food. Coincidentally, they both began in the late 1940s.

The Ownership Revolution saw working people become the owners of big corporations in many countries. Through pension funds, mutual funds, and other retirement savings vehicles, we bought and bought until we came to dominate the world of investment.

As a result, we now receive the lion's share of income from corporate dividends, and we benefit the most when corporations buy back shares. Working people also profit when the price of stocks go up, as most have for the past 60 years.

As a result, the living standards of retirees in general have now reached a level that previous generations would consider a dream. While not everyone lives that dream, the breadth and depth of improvement overall has been breathtaking.

As we also saw, McDonald's gave us the Fast Food revolution. Grasping the spirit of Henry Ford's assembly line innovations, the McDonald brothers invented fast food as we know it today. By the 1960s, Ray Kroc had grown the little hamburger stand into a major corporation.

Through retirement savings vehicles, working people invested much of the capital that allowed McDonald's to grow from a handful of restaurants in the mid-1950s to some 35,000 today.

As McDonald's has grown, its profits have grown. Much of that profit has gone to working people as they collected and continue to collect dividends through their pension funds, mutual funds and other retirement savings vehicles.

No matter who invented or developed fast food, it seems inevitable that low costs would and must prevail. Part of that low cost, high volume strategy includes wage levels that attract criticism.

Will that ever change? Will fast food find a way to pay significantly higher wages and mute the criticism? That seems unlikely since consumers dictate how the industry prices and pays, and they like the status quo. For the foreseeable future, fast food will provide lots of entry-level jobs, but they will remain largely temporary and low paying.

Finally, putting all the players and pieces together, we come to this conclusion: the role of modern corporations is to grow retirement incomes. Whether they sell hamburgers, high tech, or hot water tanks, corporations function as agents of social progress by generating retirement incomes for seniors.

McDonald's future, as well as its iconic status, will depend on how well it continues to meet this measure of social utility. And our future and the health of our retirement income will depend, much more than we knew, on how well we choose our corporations.

Postscript

In 1929, Richard and Maurice (Dick and Mac) left New Hampshire, poor boys who hoped to make their fortune in California. And after stints as stage hands and the owner-operators of a hot dog stand and a drive-in restaurant, they found some success in the original McDonald's restaurant.

After the remake of 1948, they found the wealth they sought. That, plus the sale of their company to Ray Kroc allowed them to retire prosperously back in New Hampshire in 1970. The following year, Maurice died at the age of 69.

Richard lived on to see a thaw in the family's relationship with the corporation. In 1984, the President of McDonald's U.S.A. cooked the 50-billionth hamburger and served it to Richard at New York's Grand Hyatt hotel. Richard died in 1998, at the age of 89.

Kroc enjoyed great success at the helm of McDonald's, building a reputation and fortune that made him a pillar of the American business establishment. Despite health issues at the end of his life and his ownership of the San Diego Padres baseball team, Kroc continued to carefully watch over the organization. He died in 1984, at the age of 81. (sources for this section include: http://encyclopedia.jrank.org/articles/pages/6307/McDonald-Mac-McDonald-Dick.html (McDonalds) and http://www.entrepreneur.com/ article/ 197544 (Kroc)

Next

Big Macs & Our Pensions: Who Gets McDonald's Profits? is the first in what is expected to be a series of booklets exploring the Ownership Revolution. Please visit *http:// thenewowners.com/* for more information. If you would like to be notified of new releases, please visit the Contact page on this site and send a message.

Also by Robert F. Abbott:

Business Writing Skills: 3 Quick & Easy Improvements You can Make Today. As the title suggests, this booklet offers practical advice about communicating effectively or persuasively. You can read it and begin putting its principles to work in less than half an hour and the list price is just $2.99.

Organizational Communication Flow: How to Make the Most of Upward, Downward, & Lateral Communication in Organizations explores the way we use each of these flows and how we can make the most of them. List price $2.99.

A Manager's Guide to Newsletters: Communicating for Results. An older (2001), print book that helps managers and publishers address the business side of employee, customer, and member newsletters. it is a full-length, paperback/hard cover title.

About the Author

To give you important business, economic, and policy ideas that are easily read and understood, **Robert F. Abbott** combines his experience as a radio news writer and announcer with analytical skills gained in earning a Master of Business Administration degree.

He also used this combination of knowledge and skills to advocate for his employee and marketing newsletter clients while owning and operating The Newsletter Company. Mr. Abbott also published his own online newsletter on business communication topics from 1999 to 2006.

When not writing and publishing, Mr. Abbott is an active community volunteer, which included serving as President of the *Airdrie Festival of Lights Society*. This association manages and operates one of North America's largest outdoor holiday light spectaculars. He lives in Airdrie, Alberta, Canada where he is often dragged along dog paths by a Jack Russell Terrier just a fraction of his size.

www.ingramcontent.com/pod-product-compliance
Lightning Source LLC
Chambersburg PA
CBHW071412200326
41520CB00014B/3411